A Very Special Eraser

The Power to Repair Mistakes

Green Fig

By: Zeina El-Chaar

Illustrated By:

CHY Illustration & Design

Name:

Publisher: Green Fig
Pennsylvania, USA
www.gogreenfig.com
info@gogreenfig.com

Green Fig

Pure Hearts
Strong Minds

A Very Special Eraser - First edition
ISBN: 978-1953836687

Note to Parents:

This story is crafted to help children understand the importance of apologizing and making amends in a fun and engaging way. As you read with your child, you'll discover how a very special eraser teaches both kids and adults how to fix mistakes and strengthen relationships. Before the story, you'll find a special section with practical strategies to guide you through real-life situations where apologies and repairs are needed. We hope this book helps your family build stronger, kinder connections and find it a valuable tool to teach them how to apologize, make amends, ask for forgiveness, and accept it.

Mistakes are a natural part of all relationships, and it's common to occasionally cross boundaries or hurt the ones we love. This is especially true with our children, as stress, fatigue, and the mental load of daily life can sometimes cause us to lose patience. If you're reading this, it means you already have the desire to improve your relationship with your child while fostering their well-being.

Numerous studies show that knowing how to repair a situation is essential for emotional development and has a lasting positive impact on children. This is the art of making amends! By modeling how to make amends, parents demonstrate their sincerity and reinforce their role as a source of emotional security for their children. By applying the strategies suggested, we can model positive behaviors that encourage children to follow suit. When we make amends, we show children that mistakes can be corrected and there is always room for growth, making this book a valuable tool, not just for children, but also for parents and caregivers.

Our religion also teaches us the value of apologizing and making things right when we've wronged others. It reminds us of our responsibility to seek forgiveness and, when necessary, compensate those we have harmed. Furthermore, our faith encourages and guides us to repent sincerely when we commit sins, with the reassurance that our Merciful Lord accepts sincere repentance.

We hope this book inspires meaningful conversations and helps nurture an environment of love, forgiveness, and growth in your family.

Zeina El-Chaar M.sc. Ps.ed

Strategies for Parents & Educators:

To make amends with others, especially with children, here are some tried and effective tips and strategies for complete and positive repair:

- Have sincere intentions and speak from the heart with your child and the person involved.

- Take responsibility for your actions, name what should not have been done, and apologize: "I yelled very loudly at you, I shouldn't have done that, I'm sorry…"

- Try to understand how the child might feel: "You must have been scared or confused about what was happening."

- Reassure and explain the steps taken to resolve the situation, or what will be done if a similar situation happens again. For example: "Next time I'm angry, I will leave the room for a few minutes" or "Dad realizes he needs to work on his reactions."

- Be clear about the plan and solutions that will be tried in the future. For example: distancing oneself from the situation, taking deep breaths, talking again calmly later, asking for advice, etc.

- Show your child that they are safe and that you are handling the situation. This can be done by telling the child that you love them, they are safe, and you care for them.

- Reframe the message by naming a need or a clear request: "I'm tired... I need respect, listening, time, a break, recognition, appreciation, etc."

- Allow enough time for calming down, respecting everyone's pace. Avoid forcing hugs or physical contact to feel less guilty.

- Remember that while our child (or the other person) may have faults that require patience, they also have many qualities for which we are grateful. They are not perfect.

- Remember as well that education and change take time, practice, and repetition.

- Warning: Don't downplay the child's reactions or emotions, make excuses, or blame the child. For example: "It's because mom is tired, and you make me angry." These statements are not apologies.

- And most importantly, give yourself time and compassion. These situations happen in all families, and no interaction is perfect. Effort and good intentions go a long way, and it's not the quantity of positive interactions that matter, but their quality.

The Conflict in Amer's Class

"Finally! It's time to play!" Amer exclaimed as he quickly put away his notebooks and rushed toward the Lego table. Playtime was his favorite part of the day. His first-grade class always had a short break at the end of the day for free play.

With a big smile, Amer went straight
to the Lego corner. There were other
play areas in the classroom—the
dress-up corner, the drawing corner—
but Amer always picked Lego.

Today, several kids wanted to join
in, including Sawsan, who had a
plan to build a Ferris wheel.

"No way! We started building a truck yesterday, and I'm going to finish it!" Amer declared, his voice sharp with frustration.

Ms. Amira, their teacher, glanced over, surprised by Amer's outburst. She walked over just in time to see Amer snatch some Lego pieces from Sawsan, causing several bricks to scatter across the floor.

Ms. Amira gently pulled Amer aside. "Amer," she said softly, "let's take a moment to calm down. Take three big breaths, then tell me what happened."

Amer's eyes, still wide with surprise, began
to soften as he took deep breaths. Ms. Amira
opened her desk drawer and pulled out a large,
colorful eraser that smelled like fruit. On it, in bold
letters, were the words: **"ERASE, REPAIR, AND
MAKE THINGS RIGHT."**

"This is a special eraser," Ms. Amira explained.
"It can help fix things when we make someone
sad or upset. I think it might help you with what
happened with Sawsan."

Amer took the eraser, feeling calmer, and nodded. He walked over to Sawsan.

"Sawsan, I'm sorry I yelled and took the Lego from you." Amer said, his voice gentle. "I was just excited to finish the truck. I should've asked what you wanted to do first. Can we share the Legos?"

Sawsan smiled. "It's okay, Amer. We can do both! Want to help me build?"

Amer grinned, relieved, as they played happily together for the rest of the day.

The Evening at Amer's House

Later that evening, Amer and his family gathered to set the table for dinner. His little sister, Lina, carefully placed forks on the table, while his older sister, Sarah, sat at the table, focused on her books.

"Sarah, come help!" Lina called out.

"Okay, I'm coming," Sarah replied, her eyes still glued to the pages in front of her. But as time passed and Sarah didn't get up, Lina grew frustrated. "Mom said we all have to help! That means you too!" she said, her voice rising.

"I told you, I'm busy! Give me two minutes," Sarah shot back, matching Lina's tone. The tension grew between the two girls, but Amer quietly continued his own task.

Suddenly, Lina slammed a plate down with a loud clatter. "You never help us! You're acting like a princess who doesn't care about anyone!" she yelled.

Amer's eyes widened. Without hesitation, he reached into his pocket and pulled out the special eraser. Smiling, he handed it to Lina.

Lina stared at the eraser and read its message:

"ERASE, REPAIR, AND MAKE THINGS RIGHT."

Slowly, her anger began to melt away.

"You're right," Lina said softly to Sarah. "I shouldn't have called you a princess or said you don't help. I was just upset because it felt like you were ignoring me. I'm sorry."

Sarah looked up and smiled. "It's okay, Lina. I wasn't ignoring you, I just had a tough day at school. I accept your apology."

The girls finished setting the table, happy that they hadn't let things spiral. Later, they all sat down and enjoyed dinner as if nothing had happened. Amer smiled, grateful that the eraser had helped once again. As the family prepared for bed, the eraser sat quietly on the edge of the table.

The next morning, Amer's dad hurried to leave for work, stuffing papers into his bag. Amer noticed the eraser on the table and grabbed it with a grin.

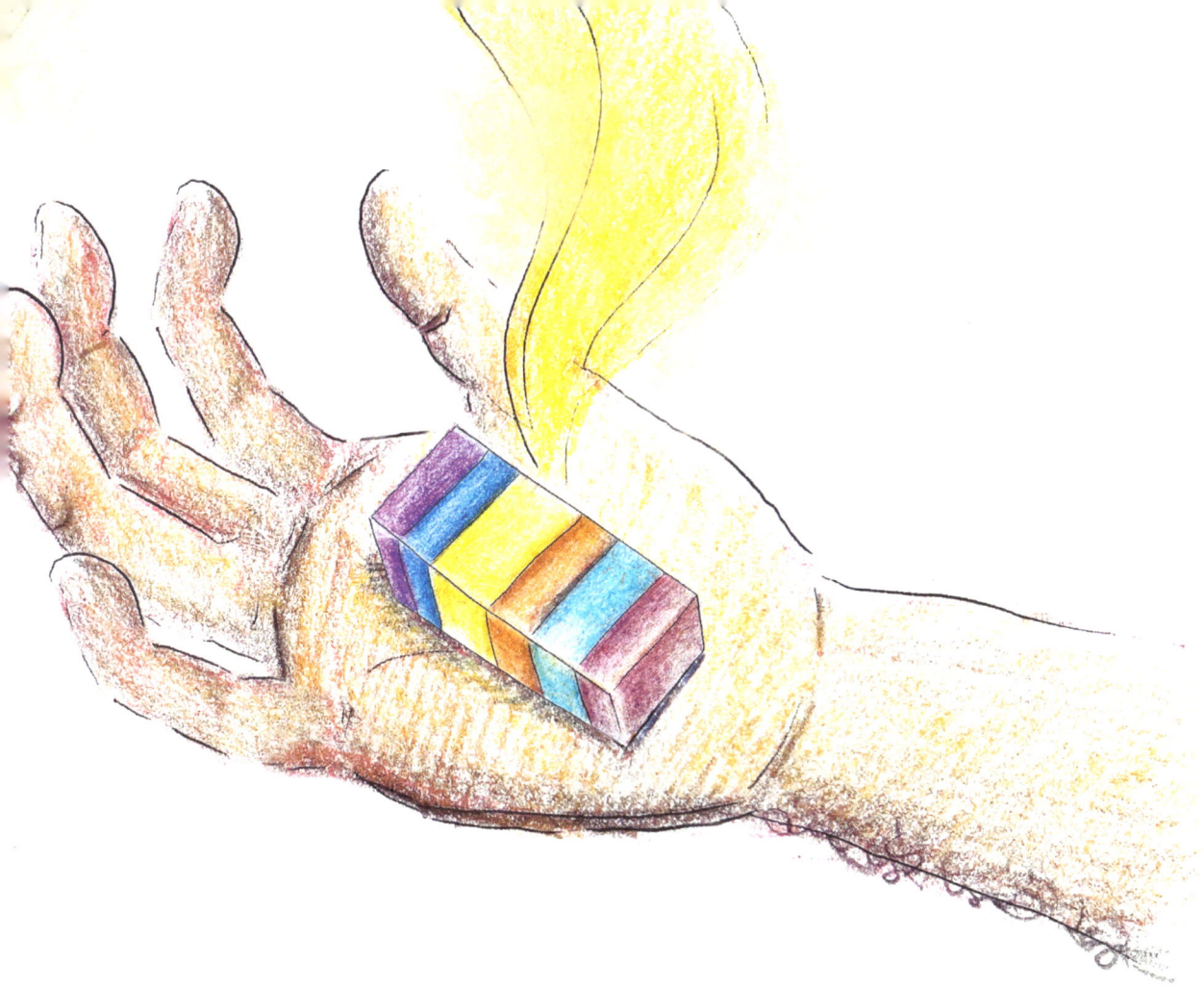

"Here, Dad!" Amer called.
"Take this with you, it might help."

His dad chuckled as he took the eraser.
"What's this? One of your secret tools?"
he teased playfully.

"Maybe," Amer replied with a wink.

And with that, Amer's dad slipped the eraser into his bag and headed off to work, unaware that it was about to help him, too.

The Incident at Amer's Dad's Workplace

At the office, things were busier than ever. Phones rang non-stop, and Amer's father worked alongside his colleague Hassan to finalize an important project. Just then, their boss stormed into the room.

"Where are the sketches? I asked for them yesterday! Why isn't this done yet?" the boss demanded, his voice booming across the office.
Amer's dad stood up calmly.
"The corrections were submitted yesterday afternoon; they're in the brown envelope on your desk!"

Embarrassed, the boss rushed back to his desk. After shuffling through papers, he found the envelope exactly where Amer's dad said it would be.

Returning to the two employees, the boss noticed the colorful eraser on the desk. With a sheepish smile, he picked it up. "Gentlemen, I'm sorry. I let my stress get the best of me. I shouldn't have spoken to you that way."

Hassan smiled. "It's okay, we understand," he replied kindly.

Amer's father chuckled while giving the eraser to his boss. "Looks like this little eraser works everywhere," he said with a grin.

The eraser sat quietly on the boss's desk, untouched, until one day, the boss picked it up, twirling it between his fingers. With a shrug, he slipped it into his briefcase and carried it home. That evening, as his son Sami rushed in from school, the boss handed him the eraser.

"Here," the boss said. "Maybe it'll come in handy for your soccer game."

During the Lively Soccer Game

Sami read the message on the eraser carefully, and thrilled to have something new, tucked it into his pocket. He grabbed his soccer ball and ran to the park. His friends were waiting for him, ready for an exciting game.

The game was intense, and Sami became focused on winning. As he dribbled toward the goal, an opponent lunged to take the ball. Determined not to lose, Sami pushed the other boy aside, causing him to stumble and fall. The ball rolled away, and the game came to an abrupt stop.

Sami's heart pounded as the boy glared at him, brushing dirt from his knees. Frustration swirled inside Sami; he didn't mean to hurt anyone, he just really wanted to win.

Suddenly, a gentle voice called out, "Young man."

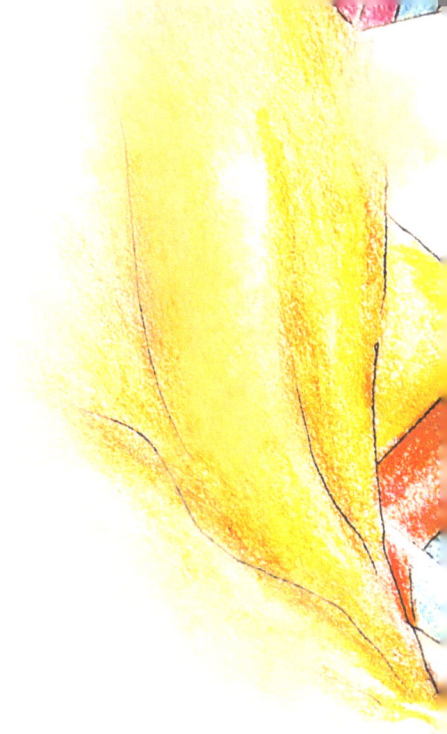

Sami turned and saw an old man sitting on a nearby bench, dressed in white and watching the children play. He recognized the man from the mosque close by. He sees him every Friday. He is the one cleaning the mosque, he is always helping and giving out candy to the kids. Sami felt a sense of relief when seeing him. The man smiled warmly and motioned for Sami to come closer.

Sami walked over. The old man placed a kind hand on Sami's shoulder. "We all make mistakes, but what matters is how we make things right. He smiled and recited a verse from the Qur'an

وَٱلْكَٰظِمِينَ ٱلْغَيْظَ وَٱلْعَافِينَ عَنِ ٱلنَّاسِ وَٱللَّهُ يُحِبُّ ٱلْمُحْسِنِينَ

Which means, "Those who restrains their anger and forgive others-surely, Allah accepts the deeds of those who do good and rewards them."

Sami sighs, responds with a smile, and nods his head. He repeats to himself what he had read on the eraser earlier: **"ERASE, REPAIR, AND MAKE THINGS RIGHT."** He puts his hand in his pocket and grips the eraser tightly.

Feeling calm, Sami returned to the boy he had pushed. "I'm sorry," Sami said softly. "I got carried away. Can we keep playing? You get the ball first."

The other boy smiled. "It's okay. Let's keep playing!"

With the game back on, Sami felt lighter, like the eraser had wiped away his mistakes. As the sun dipped lower in the sky, Sami glanced back toward the bench–but the old man was gone.

Sami smiled to himself, knowing that sometimes the biggest lesson isn't about winning–it was about kindness and making things right.

Many people had learned that lesson too, just like Sami; Amer and his sisters, his father and his coworker, and his boss at work as well.

It is never too late to learn from our mistakes and make things right.

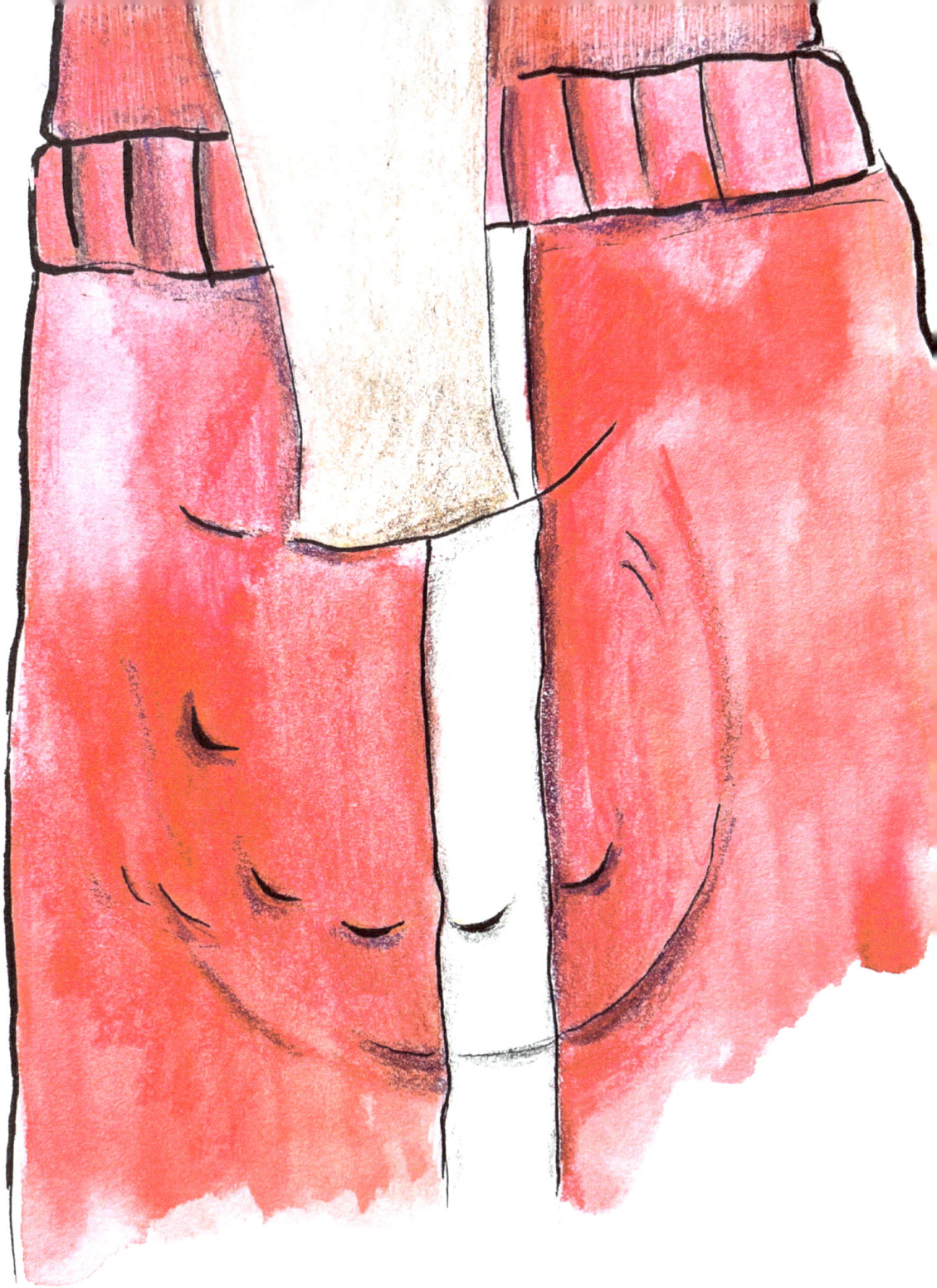

Acts of Making Amends:

- Apologize.

- Do something nice for the person.

- Help or offer a service.

- Fix the object I took or broke.

- Play with the person or spend time with them.

- Do a task on behalf of the person.

Write a letter.

Draw a picture.

Find three qualities of that person and tell them.

Give a hug if the person wants it.

Say what I will do to avoid making the same mistake again.

www.ingramcontent.com/pod-product-compliance
Lightning Source LLC
LaVergne TN
LVHW072130070426
835513LV00002B/52